Resurrection Evidences:
A Bible Study

Also by Kent Fishel (with Joel DeSelm)
Breakthrough Bible Study Series, including

Basic Christian Assurances
Basic Christian Growth
Dynamic Christian Living

Kent M. Fishel and
John W. Rayls

CORNERSTONES

Resurrection
Evidences:
A Bible Study

First in a series
of Bible studies
on the basic beliefs
of the Christian life

Lamplighter Books Grand Rapids, Michigan
Zondervan Publishing House

Zondervan Books are published by Zondervan Publishing House,
1415 Lake Drive, S.E., Grand Rapids, Michigan 49506

RESURRECTION EVIDENCES

© 1985 by The Zondervan Corporation
Grand Rapids, Michigan

Library of Congress Cataloging in Publication Data
Fishel Kent M.
   Resurrection evidences.
   (Cornerstones)
   Bibliography: p.
   1. Jesus Christ—Resurrection—Study and teaching.
2. Bible.   N.T.—Study.   I. Rayls, John W.   II. Title.
III. Series.
BT481.F53   1985   232.9'7   85-3146
ISNB 0-310-46102-2

Unless otherwise noted, all Scripture references are taken from *The Holy
Bible: New International Version* (North American Edition). Copyright © 1978
by the International Bible Society. Used by permission of the Zondervan Bible
Publishers.

Edited by Christy Elshof and Janet Kobobel
Designed by Kim Koenig
Illustrations by Louise Bauer

Printed in the United States of America

85 86 87 88 89 90 / 10 9 8 7 6 5 4 3 2 1

Introduction

Resurrection Evidences, first in a series of Bible-study books, will attempt to explain why Jesus Christ's resurrection forms the foundation of the Christian faith. While most religions teach about what happens after death, only Christianity proclaims a living Redeemer—one who died, was buried, and rose again on the third day. Without Jesus' resurrection, the entire basis of the Christian faith is destroyed.

This book will not only give the reader an understanding of the importance of the Resurrection but also show proof that Jesus Christ's resurrection is a historical event.

Jesus' resurrection brings to each believer the assurance

that through the Son of God's death on the cross, he or she, by faith, can receive forgiveness of sins and eternal life.

We suggest that you do one Bible study each day. Find a quiet spot, free from distractions. You will need a pencil and a Bible in a translation you can understand; if you want to match the phrasing of the translation used in this study, use the *New International Version*. Ask God to reveal Himself to you as you spend time with Him.

The Cornerstone series can be challenging when used on an individual basis or in a small group. For maximum effectiveness the following format is suggested: Read the verse at the top of the page. Then read through the devotional, considering how the Scripture passage relates to the questions. Answer the questions honestly and openly. By applying this study to your life, you will internalize and personalize the truths from God's word.

Make no mistake—Jesus Christ's resurrection is the core of the Christian faith. As William E. Hordern states in his book *A Layman's Guide to Protestant Theology*, for the first Christians it was impossible to be Christian and not believe in the literal bodily resurrection of Jesus. The same is true today.

Our prayer is that this Resurrection study will challenge you to examine seriously Christ's claims and then to make a decision based on the facts that have been presented.

In His Love,

Kent and John

Day 1

If a man dies, will he live again?

Job 14:14

In the above Scripture, Job asks a question that all of us think about: Is there life after death? Obviously, not everyone believes there is. Still, at one time or another everyone wonders what happens when the body dies.

The Bible teaches that life after death is a reality. In Matthew 25:46, Jesus says that unbelievers will go away to _____ _____, but the righteous to _____ _____ . In 1 John 5:11–13, we read that if anyone has the Son of God, that person has life (eternal); but if a person does not have the _____

_____ _____ , then that person does not have life (eternal). (See also John 5:24.)

The Apostle Paul, on the road to Damascus, gained a knowledge of who Jesus Christ is and learned how Jesus provides eternal life for all believers. With this personal knowledge, he addressed (in 1 Corinthians 15) some in the Corinthian church who were denying the Resurrection. Paul knew these people were in error; he also knew that denying Jesus Christ's resurrection destroys the reality of the Christian faith. Therefore, Paul began that part of his letter by giving evidence to prove that Jesus did indeed die and did rise from the grave. Paul answered the Corinthians' false beliefs with apologetics.

People at church retreats and Christian schools are often asked to define the term *apologetics.* "Apologizing for your faith" and "the science of making up excuses for what one believes" are definitions sometimes given. But Christians don't need to make up excuses for what they believe. As you study this book, you will gain insight into how to take an effective stand for what you believe by using apologetics. *Apologetics* means "giving a logical and reasonable defense of your faith."

List three reasons why you believe Jesus Christ's resurrection is true:

1. _____

2. _____

3. _____

Don't be discouraged if you couldn't list three reasons; before you finish *Resurrection Evidences,* you'll be able to list many more.

Day 2

But if it is preached that Christ has been raised from the dead, how can some of you say that there is no resurrection of the dead? If there is no resurrection of the dead, then not even Christ has been raised. And if Christ has not been raised, our preaching is useless and so is your faith. More than that, we are then found to be false witnesses about God, for we have testified about God that he raised Christ from the dead. But he did not raise him if in fact the dead are not raised. For if the dead are not raised, then Christ has not been raised either. And if Christ has not been raised, your faith is futile; you are still in your sins. Then those also who have fallen asleep in Christ are lost. If only for this life we have hope in Christ, we are to be pitied more than all men.

1 Corinthians 15:12–19

If Jesus Christ is not who He claimed to be and resurrection can never take place, then, as Paul states in 1 Corinthians 15:13, not even _____ has been raised. Verse 14 says that if this is true, then preaching is useless and so is your _____. Moreover, verse 15 states you are found to be _____ _____ about God. In verse 17 Paul declares that if Christ has not been _____ , your

13

faith is _____ ; you are still in your _____ .
Finally in verse 19, Paul says, "If only for this life we have
_____ in Christ, we are to be _____ more
than all men."

In verse 20, however, Paul boldly proclaims that Christ has
indeed been raised from the dead. Then in verse 21, you
learn that death comes through a man. (Look up verse 22.)
Who is this man through whom we experience death?
_____ . Here you learn that the resurrection of the
dead comes also through a man. Who is the man who
provides life for all mankind? _____ .

To be dead in Adam means: _____

_____

_____

To be alive in Christ means: _____

_____

_____

According to 1 Corinthians 15:58, Christians (see Appendix A for a complete understanding of what it means to be a
Christian) are to stand _____ ; they are not to let
anything move them. As a Christian, you will be able to
stand firm as you begin to understand the apologetics of
your Christian faith (the logical and reasonable explanations of your Christianity). While the Christian faith involves
the birth, life, teachings, miracles, and death of Jesus, all of
these have value and meaning only through His resurrection. If the Resurrection never took place, these other events
are meaningless.

However, it is important that you understand that there is
an abundance of evidence that Jesus Christ *did* rise from the
dead and that He is who He claims to be. As you study the

14

Resurrection, the truth of these facts will help establish your faith.

What questions do you have about the Resurrection?

1. _____

2. _____

3. _____

List three reasons people give for not believing in the Resurrection.

1. _____

2. _____

3. _____

Read on to find out why these opinions are false.

Day 3

But sanctify Christ as Lord in your hearts, always being ready to make a defense to every one who asks you to give an account for the hope that is in you, yet with gentleness and reverence.

1 Peter 3:15 NAS

Peter states that you should be able to make a _____ to everyone who asks for an account of the _____ that is in you. The information contained in this Bible study will help you share your faith with others.

Making a defense of your faith is not an option but a command, as Peter wrote in his letter to Christians. James S. Stewart, a professor of New Testament at Regents College, states, "The greatest threat to the Church is not communism, atheism, materialism; the greatest threat is Christians trying to sneak into heaven incognito without ever sharing their

16

faith." Think about what you communicate as you share your faith, and answer the following questions:

1. Christ's _____ is/are the very foundation(s) of Christianity.
   a. birth
   b. death and resurrection
   c. miracles
   d. teaching
2. Jesus said He would _____ on the third day after His death.

3. Why is Christ's resurrection important? _____

   _____

   _____

If you had difficulty with question 3, think about this statement made by a noted atheist (someone who doesn't believe there is a God): "There is no possibility whatsoever of reconciling science and theology, at least in Christendom. Either Jesus rose from the dead or He didn't. If He did, then Christianity becomes plausible; if He did not, it is sheer nonsense."

The diagram on the next page conveys the importance of the Resurrection to the Christian faith. As you can see, all of Christianity rests on two basic assertions:

1. Jesus Christ's resurrection is true.
2. The Bible is accurate and true.

These two assertions are the pillars on which the Christian faith rests. Throughout history, when an all-out attack was made on Christianity, it was directed at these two statements. Even non-Christians recognize the importance of these pillars.

17

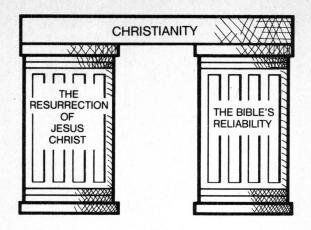

Day 4

Yet to all who received him, to those who believed in his name, he gave the right to become children of God.

John 1:12

If someone were to ask you what it means "to believe in" someone or something, what would you say?

_____

_____

_____

Everyone believes in something. Most people would admit they believe in the existence of the solar system. Some might even say they believe in the Washington Redskins, Mom, and apple pie. But what is the difference between believing in these things and believing in what John talks about in the above Scripture?

_____

_____

_____

It's easy to say the words "I believe" without placing much faith in them. People might mean different things when they use the word *believe.* Webster defines *believe* several ways. For the purpose of this Bible study, however, we will use the meaning "to expect or hope for with confidence."

The drawing on page 19 helps to illustrate. Imagine you have been in the desert for three days without water. Nearly dead, you stumble across an old-fashioned water pump. Slung over the pump is a canteen with a small amount of water and a sign directing you to prime the pump by dumping the water into the pump.

Would you believe the sign and dump the water into the pump? What kind of belief would such action take?

_____

_____

_____

If you didn't believe the sign and drank even the little bit of water from the canteen, you would eventually die of thirst. The kind of belief necessary for you to receive all the water you need and to survive would be a belief of total commitment.

After all, it would be scary to dump the only water you had seen for days down an old, dry-looking pump. Yet that very action is the only thing that can save you. When a hand pump is properly primed, the water from the well is pumped easily, and there is more than enough to quench the thirst of many people. But when the pump is not properly primed, pumping all day long will bring up no water.

This story is an example of what John means by the word "believe." He states that those who have believed (or put their confidence and trust in) Jesus, have become Christians (see Appendix A).

Day 5

After his suffering, he showed himself to these men and gave many convincing proofs that he was alive. He appeared to them over a period of forty days and spoke about the kingdom of God.

Acts 1:3

You should have a good idea now of what it means to believe in Christ. It means placing your complete trust and confidence in Him. This involves faith, but it's not a blind leap. It's acting on the evidence. The Scripture above states that Jesus presented many _____ proofs of His resurrection. During your lifetime, you'll probably be asked many times to provide proof of the "hope that lies within you."

But before you start looking at the proofs of what you believe, there are two important questions to ask:

1. What type of proof is needed?
2. How much proof is necessary?

Without answering these two questions, a discussion about proof could go on forever with no apparent solution.

To answer the first question, you need to realize there are two types of proof. One is known as *scientific proof.* This seems to be a popular phrase of the electronic generation. Many people believe that everything can and must be proven scientifically. These people believe that evidence is more important if it's labeled "scientific." Define your understanding of scientific proof.

_____

_____

_____

Scientific proof is any proof that is repeatable in a controlled environment. This leaves out many events because they are not repeatable and cannot be watched in a controlled environment. However, just because something cannot be proven scientifically doesn't mean that it's not true. For instance, you can't prove scientifically that Abraham Lincoln was the sixteenth president of the United States. Why not?

_____

_____

_____

It's not repeatable, is it? You can't go back in history and watch Lincoln become president again. Yet it's absolutely true.

Taking this one step further, you can't prove scientifically that you exist. You can't go back and be born again physically.

Obviously, there must be some other type of proof that is just as valid as scientific proof. It's *legal-historical proof.* This consists of public records: birth certificates, death certificates, and any other legal records. With this type of proof, it would be easy to prove your existence or that Lincoln was the sixteenth president of the United States. The same is true for the resurrection of Christ. You can examine legal-historical proofs, which is what you'll do in the rest of this book.

Day 6

"Come now, let us reason together," says the LORD. "Though your sins are like scarlet, they shall be as white as snow; though they are red as crimson, they shall be like wool."

Isaiah 1:18

According to our criminal-justice system, you must prove a defendant guilty beyond a _____ doubt.

If you didn't answer, "beyond a *reasonable* doubt," then your answer was incorrect. This doesn't mean that you are ignorant; you've probably been watching too much TV. Unfortunately, the media have programmed you to think that guilt must be proven one hundred percent. This isn't the case. A decision by a judge concerning the guilt or innocence of a defendant doesn't rest on the absence of *any* doubt but on the evidence at hand.

In a civil-court case, you only need to have _____ percent of the evidence in your favor to win a judgment. A simple majority of the facts will win your case. A legal term for this is "preponderance of the evidence." Obviously, this leaves a lot of room for doubt—in fact, forty-nine-percent doubt; a verdict will be handed down based on the fifty-one percent of the evidence that favors one side or the other.

In addition to our court system asking only for evidence beyond a reasonable doubt, you make the same type of decisions everyday. For instance, do you ever ask for one-hundred-percent proof that the food you eat is safe? To get one-hundred-percent proof, you might feed some of each food to mice and watch to see if anything happens to them. Or you might hire an official food tester. However, even with these precautions, you'll not have one-hundred-percent proof that your food is safe.

Other areas of life in which you may make assumptions about safety include the water you drink, the furniture on which you sit, and even the air you breathe. No one can say with one-hundred-percent certainty that these aspects of life are safe. However, these assumptions are extremely important every day of your life.

It should be easy to see that it's not reasonable to demand one-hundred-percent proof of anything. Since our court system judges the guilt or innocence of a man based on reasonable doubt and our decisions on the essentials of life are based on the same, how can you demand more concerning Christ's resurrection? You'll find the evidence for His resurrection is more than enough to convince anyone beyond a reasonable doubt. This doesn't mean that you can expect the absence of all doubt but rather that the available evidence overwhelmingly supports the literal resurrection of Jesus Christ.

Read Luke 5:4–11. In this passage, you learn that Jesus told Simon to put his boat out into deep water and then to

26

lower the fishing nets. Before Simon put the fishing nets into the water, he explained to Jesus that he and his fellow fishermen had been fishing all _____ and had caught _____ . But because Jesus told him to do it, Simon obeyed.

Being a trained and experienced fisherman, Simon must have wondered about the advice Jesus gave. He knew that men never went fishing at that spot that time of day because there were no fish to catch. He was also aware that his friends, who were nearby, would laugh at him for listening to a religious prophet's fishing advice. In spite of these doubts, however, Simon believed beyond a reasonable doubt in what Jesus said and acted upon his belief. As you can see, according to Luke 5:6–7, the results were astonishing. Simon caught such a great number of fish that the nets _____ .

Many people have doubts about the safety of flying; yet thousands of people board airplanes every day and fly all over the world. Most of these people can't explain how the planes fly. In fact, it seems illogical that a plane can even get into the air. But despite their hesitations, people who fly are convinced beyond a reasonable doubt that flying is a safe mode of transportation.

Can you name three other areas in which people generally have doubts but proceed because of the weight of the evidence?

1. _____

2. _____

3. _____

Day 7

Then why, you may be asking, did I change my plan? Hadn't I really made up my mind yet? Or am I like a man of the world who says "yes" when he really means "no"? Never! As surely as God is true, I am not that sort of person. My "yes" means "yes." Timothy and Silvanus and I have been telling you about Jesus Christ the Son of God. He isn't one to say "yes" when he means "no." He always does exactly what he says.

2 Corinthians 1:17–19 LB

Write in your own words what Paul teaches in 2 Corinthians 1:17–19.

_____

_____

_____

_____

_____

Many people in our world today want to compromise the truth; they base their responses to others on what they think people want them to say. Their "yes" and "no" depend totally on fitting in with the crowd and not on their personal values.

Paul states in 2 Corinthians 1:18 that his word is not _____ and _____ . He is saying that as a Christian his words are always to be the truth, no matter what others say or expect him to say.

After you read James 5:12, write down what James admonishes the reader to do.

_____

_____

_____

From a logical point of view, why is it important that you speak the truth in love rather than just sharing the popular view or trying to say what others expect you to say?

_____

_____

_____

The answer to this question is found in a simple communication principle known as the *Law of Noncontradiction*. This law states that if there are two contradictory statements, one of them is true or both are false. In other words, both statements can't be true. The Law of Noncontradiction is the basis for all truthful and meaningful communication. Without this law, there can be no effective communication between people.

An example of this law would be these two statements:

1. Baseballs are round.
2. Baseballs are square.

One of these statements is true or both are false. According to the Law of Noncontradiction, both statements can't be true because they contradict each other.

Can you think of another set of statements as an example? (Remember that the two statements must truly contradict each other.)

1. _____

2. _____

The resurrection of Jesus Christ is not a "maybe yes" or a "maybe no" situation. Based on the Law of Noncontradiction, Jesus either rose from the dead or He didn't. (Either baseballs are round or they aren't.) Both can't be true.

Day 8

And when the centurion, who stood there in front of Jesus, heard his cry and saw how he died, he said, "Surely this man was the Son of God!"

Mark 15:39

Jesus was both God and man at the same time. Jesus had existed forever as God but was born of a virgin as a man. He walked, ate, and drank just like everyone else. Christ, as a man, was tempted in the same ways you are. The big difference is that He lived His life without once giving in to sin. Read Hebrews 4:15. Write your understanding of what it means that Jesus was "tempted in every way."

_____

_____

Match the letter in front of the Scripture passage with Jesus' human trait.

a. Isaiah 7:14   _____ He was thirsty.

b. Luke 2:52   _____ He was the carpenter's son.

c. Matthew 13:55   _____ He cried.

d. Matthew 15:32   _____ He suffered physically.

e. John 11:35   _____ He ate and drank.

f. John 13:1   _____ He was tempted in every
                              way just as we are.

g. 1 Peter 4:1   _____ He was conceived and a
                              woman gave birth to Him.

h. Phil. 2:8   _____ He had compassion on the
                              crowds.

i. Matthew 11:19   _____ He grew mentally and
                              physically.

j. Hebrews 2:18   _____ He loved the disciples.

k. Hebrews 4:15   _____ He was in a man's body
                              when He died.

l. Isaiah 53:3   _____ He suffered when He was
                              tempted.

m. John 19:28   _____ He was in mental anguish.

n. Luke 22:44   _____ He could do nothing by
                              Himself but needed God
                              the Father.

o. John 5:30   _____ He was a man of sorrows,
                              familiar with grief.

According to Mark 15:39, the centurion saw Jesus as a man and even possibly as the _____ _____ . Joseph of _____ in Mark 15:43 asked for the body of Jesus. Then, in Mark 15:44–45, Pilate, after asking the centurion if Jesus was really _____ , gave Jesus' body to Joseph. Historians agree that Jesus Christ was crucified and buried and that His tomb was found empty. These facts stand; they are based on the biblical accounts and on such historical writings as Josephus' *Antiquities of the Jews* and Suetonius' *Life of Claudius*. Disagreement arises, however, about why Jesus' tomb was empty on Easter morning.

Day 9

He answered, "A wicked and adulterous generation asks for a miraculous sign! But none will be given it except the sign of the prophet Jonah. For as Jonah was three days and three nights in the belly of a huge fish, so the Son of Man will be three days and three nights in the heart of the earth."

Matthew 12:39—40

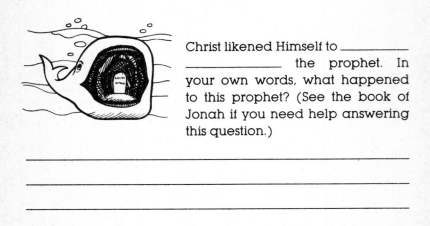

Christ likened Himself to _____ _____ the prophet. In your own words, what happened to this prophet? (See the book of Jonah if you need help answering this question.)

_____

_____

_____

_____

What truth did Jesus teach the scribes and Pharisees about Himself?

_____

_____

_____

_____

In what ways was Jesus like Jonah?

_____

_____

_____

_____

Jesus declared the same idea in John 2:19, when he referred to Himself as the _____ . Again in Mark 8:31, Christ predicted not only His death but also His resurrection. As you can see, Jesus taught His disciples, the religious leaders, and the Jews about His death and resurrection.

Some critics claim that Christ never said He would rise from the dead. A few of these people have said that Jesus never taught others about a literal bodily resurrection. Read Matthew 27:62–63. In these verses, the chief priests and Pharisees were with Pilate and claimed that Jesus said He would _____ after three days. This clearly indicates that the Jewish leaders understood that Jesus was speaking of a literal bodily resurrection.

Day 10

Give the order for the tomb to be made secure until the third day. Otherwise, his disciples may come and steal the body and tell the people that he has been raised from the dead. This last deception will be worse than the first.

Matthew 27:64

The Jewish leaders were concerned about guarding the tomb of Jesus for three days. What did they fear would happen if His body disappeared?

_____

_____

_____

_____

Since these Jewish leaders had tried unsuccessfully for

three years to belittle, shame, and do away with Jesus, they wanted to take no chance that His body would be moved or stolen. According to Matthew 27:66, to insure that the grave was secure, the Jewish leaders: (circle one)

    a. sent other leaders.
    b. went themselves.
    c. sent a guard.
    d. installed a TV camera.

They took three specific steps to make sure Jesus' body would not disappear. (See Matthew 27:60–66.)

    1. A great _____ was rolled in front of the tomb to block the entrance.
    2. A set of _____ were placed at the entrance to the tomb.
    3. A wax _____ was placed on the stone blocking the entrance.

These three actions, plus the common knowledge that the death penalty was given anyone tampering with a grave, made it extremely difficult for the body to disappear.

In preparation for tomorrow's Bible study, look up Luke 24:7, and write down what Jesus said about His death and resurrection before the Crucifixion took place.

_____

_____

_____

_____

Why is it significant that Jesus predicted these happenings before He died?

Day 11

He is not here; he has risen, just as he said. Come and see the place where he lay.

Matthew 28:6

After the Jewish Sabbath had ended, some women came to Jesus' tomb to anoint His body with spices (Mark 16:1). When they arrived at the tomb, an angel explained to them why it was empty. From the account in Matthew 28:6, write down why Jesus' tomb was empty:

_____

_____

_____

These women certainly were not expecting such news. In fact, Mark 16:3 states that they were concerned about who would move the _____ for them when they arrived at the tomb. Furthermore, in John's account (John 20:1–2), you see that Mary had no idea why the tomb was empty as she shared the news with some of the _____.

In addition to the women's conclusion, you learn in John 20:3–10 that the disciples: (circle one)

    a. knew Jesus had risen from the dead.
    b. knew someone had stolen Jesus' body.
    c. thought the women had been drinking.
    d. didn't understand that Jesus had risen from the dead.

As a matter of fact, all four Gospels mention the surprise and confusion on the part of Christ's friends and followers. All these historical accounts agree that the tomb was empty.
Give four possible explanations for why Jesus' tomb was empty:

1. _____

2. _____

3. _____

4. _____

Before you read any further, summarize in your own words why you think Jesus claimed to be God—who forgave sins, performed miracles, foretold His death and resurrection, and rose from the grave.

_____

Day 12

No, we speak of God's secret wisdom, a wisdom that has been hidden and that God destined for our glory before time began. None of the rulers of this age understood it, for if they had, they would not have crucified the Lord of glory.

1 Corinthians 2:7—8

Today most people would describe a wise person as someone who: _____

_____

_____

_____

But true wisdom begins with what (Proverbs 9:10)?

_____

_____

_____

God deliberately made the gift of salvation so simple that it would confuse and confound those who claim, from a human or worldly standpoint, to be wise.

After reading 1 Corinthians 2:7–8, note in verse 8 that if the Jewish leaders of Jesus' day would have understood God's wisdom, they would not have _____ Jesus.

It's with this same worldly wisdom that men and women today try to present reasons why Christ's tomb was empty rather than accept the simple and clear evidences concerning His resurrection.

Most people who argue against Christ's resurrection have a world view that doesn't include God. Therefore, they automatically conclude that the biblical account of Christ's resurrection can't be logical. This is known as "presuppositional thinking," which means "my mind is made up; don't confuse me with the facts!" How does 1 Corinthians 2:14 describe this kind of person and his or her understanding of spiritual things?

_____

_____

_____

In the next few Bible studies, you'll study the four main explanations people give for Christ's empty tomb. They are:

1. Jesus never actually died.
2. Mary and the disciples went to the wrong tomb.
3. Someone stole the body.
4. Jesus actually rose from the dead.

Is your mind open to study the facts about the empty tomb? _____ (yes/no) If you aren't open, explain why.

_____

_____

_____

If you desire to know the truth about the tomb, then, according to Isaiah 1:18, you need to _____ together with the Lord. This means you will _____

_____

_____

Day 13

The soldiers therefore came and broke the legs of the first man who had been crucified with Jesus, and then those of the other. But when they came to Jesus and found that he was already dead, they did not break His legs.

John 19:32–33

One of the explanations for the empty tomb is called the *Swoon Theory.* This theory states that Jesus Christ never actually died but simply fainted, or swooned. As you read and study John 19:32–33, state why you think the soldiers didn't break the legs of Jesus.

_____

_____

_____

Luke 23:46 (read also Matthew 27:50) mentions that Jesus made a final statement and then "he _____ his last." This is another way of saying that Jesus died. Also notice that in Mark 15:44–45 Pilate heard directly from the _____ that Jesus was _____. He then gave the body to Joseph.

John Stott, in his book *Basic Christianity,* relates that the centurion was very familiar with how to know if a person was dead. Due to the harshness of Roman military discipline, the centurion didn't take lightly the task of ascertaining the time of death of his prisoner.

You have just read four different accounts of this same event, all agreeing that Jesus Christ died on the cross. Write down what you believe actually caused death during a crucifixion.

_____

_____

_____

Dr. Henry Halley, in his book *Halley's Bible Handbook,* explains that a person who was hung on a cross died a slow and agonizing death. Halley states, "Nails were driven through the hands and feet, the victim was left hanging there in agony, starvation, insufferable thirst, and excruciating convulsions of pain. Death usually followed in four to six days." Death was brought about by a combination of all of those things, but primarily by suffocation. The body's weight pulled down on the outstretched limbs, resulting in stress on the rib cage. It became increasingly difficult to expand the lungs enough to draw in fresh oxygen. If the people in charge of the crucifixion became bored or just wanted to speed up the death process, they broke the legs of the condemned person. This prevented the criminal from pressing his heels against the cross's upright post and arching his back to expand his diaphragm. (See *The Resurrection Factor* by Josh McDowell.)

From John 19:33 you learn that the soldiers didn't break Christ's legs because they knew He was already _____ . What prophecy did this fulfill (Psalms 34:20)?

_____

According to 1 Peter 3:18, why do you think Jesus had to die?

_____

_____

_____

Day 14

Instead, one of the soldiers pierced Jesus' side with a spear, bringing a sudden flow of blood and water.

John 19:34

There are many factors to examine when you are considering the truthfulness of the *Swoon Theory*.

First, to accept this theory you must establish that Jesus managed to live through some of the most brutal and inhumane treatment ever inflicted on a person. Match the following Scriptures with the descriptions given of Jesus' treatment prior to and while hanging on the cross.

a. Isaiah 50:6   _____ Pilate had Jesus flogged.

b. Isaiah 52:14   _____ Soldiers pierced Jesus' side.

c. Matthew 26:67-68   _____ Jesus was spit on and struck on the head.

d. Matthew 27:29   _____ Jesus' beard was pulled out.

e. Matthew 27:30   _____ One of the officers struck Jesus' face.

f. Mark 15:15   _____ A crown of thorns was pressed on His head.

g. John 18:22   _____ Jesus' appearance was disfigured and marred.

h. John 19:34   _____ He was spit on, beaten, and slapped while blindfolded.

In preparation for the crucifixion, Pilate had Jesus flogged. This was a brutal and painful ordeal. A leather whip laced with pieces of pottery and metal was used. This whip peeled the flesh and muscle tissue away from the body with each lash so that the victim's back and legs were left in shreds.

After this, the victim was forced to walk (and many times carry the crossbar of the cross) to the place of crucifixion. There he was nailed to the crossbar. Then he was either hoisted up and fastened to the already standing post or the entire cross with the person nailed to it was lifted up and dropped into a hole. This process alone was enough to make death appear appealing to the one being crucified.

Jesus underwent all of the above, and then in John 19:34 you read that one of the soldiers _____ His side. Dr. John Isch (head of the division of Cardiovascular-Thoracic Surgery at the St. Vincent Medical Center in Indianapolis, Indiana) states that the blood and water flowing down from the side of Christ (John 19:34) indicates a high probability

49

of death. All of this evidence would point overwhelmingly to the fact that Jesus actually died on the cross.

As you conclude today's study, list the reasons given for Christ's sufferings found in Isaiah 53:4—6.

_____

_____

_____

Day 15

Joseph took the body, wrapped it in a clean linen cloth, and placed it in his own new tomb that he had cut out of the rock. He rolled a big stone in front of the entrance to the tomb and went away.

Matthew 27:59—60

The next major obstacle to believing the *Swoon Theory* is the historical evidence of the extensive grave preparations. From reading today's Scripture, write down the two things that were done for Christ's burial in Joseph's tomb:

1. _____

2. _____

The normal practice of the time was to wrap a dead body in one hundred to two hundred pounds of graveclothes and spices. Professor James Hastings (as quoted by Josh McDowell in *Evidence That Demands a Verdict*) points out that the use of myrrh on dead bodies before they were wrapped caused the clothes to adhere closely to the body, making it almost impossible to remove the grave wrappings.

Jesus received no medical attention for His wounds; He had lost much blood; and He was placed in a cool, damp tomb. If Jesus were somehow still alive (the essence of the *Swoon Theory*) and didn't die of pneumonia, then He would certainly die from suffocation due to the weight of the grave-clothes and spices.

Even if someone believed that Jesus was not dead after this burial process, that person would still have to explain how Jesus, in this weakened condition, could move a boulder that weighed, according to historians' estimates, between two thousand and four thousand pounds.

In addition, Matthew 27:65–66 explains that a _____ was placed at the tomb. If Jesus could have rolled away the stone, then He still would have had to encounter the guards, who would have stopped Him at any cost.

How much faith does it take to believe the *Swoon Theory* as you know it so far? Shade in the graph on the next page to indicate your answer.

UNSWERVING FAITH

STRONG FAITH

FAIR AMOUNT OF FAITH

A LITTLE FAITH

NOT MUCH FAITH

Day 16

On the evening of that first day of the week, when the disciples were together, with the doors locked for fear of the Jews, Jesus came and stood among them and said, "Peace be with you!"

John 20:19

To believe the *Swoon Theory*, you must accept that Jesus never actually died in spite of receiving severe beatings, having a crown of thorns placed on His head, being scourged, being nailed to a cross, being hung in the air, and having a spear thrust into His side. You must accept that the Roman soldiers, Jewish leaders, and Pilate himself didn't know what a dead man looked like and weren't concerned enough to make sure. You must accept that Christ freed Himself from His grave-clothes after He had revived from His "faint." You must accept that after accomplishing this spectacular feat, Jesus

54

then moved a rock weighing between one to two tons, and scared away the Roman guards stationed in front of the tomb. Finally, for you to believe the *Swoon Theory,* you must accept that Jesus walked several miles to where His disciples were and then convinced them that He had a wonderful new body and that they could have one like it. If His body were not a miraculously new one, who of the disciples would have wanted one like it?

What is your explanation of John 20:19–20? How could Jesus appear to the disciples inside a room when the doors were shut and locked?

_____

_____

_____

In your own words, write why you believe the *Swoon Theory* to be false.

_____

_____

_____

_____

Day 17

Do not think that I have come to abolish the Law or the Prophets; I have not come to abolish them but to fulfill them. I tell you the truth, until heaven and earth disappear, not the smallest letter, not the least stroke of a pen, will by any means disappear from the Law until everything is accomplished.

Matthew 5:17–18

 An offshoot of the original *Swoon Theory* was brought to the public's attention in the late 1960s when Hugh Schoenfield wrote a book called *The Passover Plot*. Schoenfield, along with a few other critics of the literal resurrection, added a new twist to the *Swoon Theory*. They suggested that prior to His death, Jesus had hoped to make great political gains by faking His death on the cross and then appearing to come to life again. In this way, Jesus could fool the people into believing that He was God's appointed leader to free the Jewish people from their bondage to the Romans.

However, Schoenfield and these other critics said that Jesus' deceptive plan failed when the soldier thrust a spear into Jesus' side.

But Jesus emphasized to His disciples, the Jewish leaders, and the Jewish people the importance of *all* prophecies being fulfilled to prove His credibility. In the above Scripture, Jesus taught that not the smallest letter of prophecy or law would pass away until _____ is accomplished. In addition to the earlier arguments you studied against the *Swoon Theory*, the number of prophecies Jesus Christ accurately fulfilled must be examined.

Peter Stoner in his book *Science Speaks* states that the probability of eight of the Old Testament prophecies being fulfilled in one man would be 1×10^{17}, which is one chance in 100,000,000,000,000,000. Stoner goes on to say the possibility of this happening would be the same as burying the State of Texas two feet deep in silver dollars with one of these dollars painted black. Then, after blindfolding someone and telling him that he can walk anywhere in Texas, this person must *on the first try* pick up the black silver dollar.

As difficult as it is to imagine anyone accidentally fulfilling eight prophecies, try to imagine someone accidentally fulfilling over three hundred. According to Josh McDowell in his book *More Than a Carpenter*, Christ fulfilled sixty major prophecies and two hundred and seventy related prophecies.

What do you think is the significance of more than three hundred prophecies being fulfilled through Jesus Christ's life, death, and resurrection?

_____

_____

Day 18

Joseph took the body, wrapped it in a clean linen cloth, and placed it in his own new tomb that he had cut out of the rock. He rolled a big stone in front of the entrance to the tomb and went away. Mary Magdalene and the other Mary were sitting there opposite the tomb.

Matthew 27:59–61

The second major alternative to believing in a literal bodily resurrection of Jesus Christ is the *Wrong Tomb* theory. This theory states that the women, Joseph of Arimathea, the Jewish leaders, and many others all went to the wrong tomb searching for Jesus' body.

This theory suggests that the women, in their grief over the recent crucifixion of a loved one, became confused and disoriented when they arrived at the grave. This theory proposes that rather than actually talking to an angel (see Mark 16:5–7 for the biblical account), the women talked to the gardener. He told them that Jesus wasn't buried in that tomb but in one that was close by. Furthermore, this view states that because of their confusion, these women misunderstood the gardener. They thought he said Jesus was alive and no longer in the tomb. Matthew 27:61 states that _____ and the other _____ were at the grave during the burial. Obviously, these women would have recognized the original site of Jesus' tomb since they had been there before.

Second, in Matthew 27:59–60, you are told that Jesus' tomb belonged to a rich man, Joseph of Arimathea. At least one person knew the exact location of the tomb. Obviously, when the women claimed that Christ had risen from the dead, Joseph of Arimathea could have taken the women to the right tomb.

Finally, remember all the trouble the Jewish leaders took to insure Jesus' death. Can you imagine these same leaders forgetting where the body was buried, especially in light of Matthew 27:63? In review, according to this verse what was the Jewish leaders' greatest fear concerning Christ's body?

_____

It's difficult to believe that the Jewish leaders, when they heard of the disappearance of Jesus' body, went to the wrong tomb. They had seen to it that guards were placed in front of the tomb and that the official Roman seal was placed on the stone.

Moreover, if the *Wrong Tomb* theory were correct, only one item had to be produced to destroy this newly formed religion. What was it?

_____

The absence of this item serves as a powerful proof for the Resurrection—Jesus Christ's body was never produced. In your opinion, what is the most glaring weakness of the *Wrong Tomb* theory?

_____

_____

_____

_____

Day 19

His appearance was like lightning, and his clothes were white as snow. The guards were so afraid of him that they shook and became like dead men.

Matthew 28:3−4

The most popular theory opposing the Resurrection is that of the *Stolen Body.* This theory states that someone or some group stole Jesus' body to gain political and religious control in Palestine.

Most people believe there were three groups that had the desire and motivation to steal the body. Who do you think these there groups were?

1. J _____ L _____
2. R _____
3. D _____

Why would the Jewish leaders steal the body?

_____

_____

_____

The *Stolen Body* theory says that the Jewish leaders might have moved the body to prevent its theft by the disciples or to bring even more grief and humiliation to Christ's followers. However, assuming these statements are correct, you are still confronted with this fact: All the Jewish authorities had to do to stop Jesus' followers from preaching about the Resurrection was to produce the body.

You have the same problem in trying to develop a reason why the Roman authorities would steal Jesus' body. Obviously, if they wanted the body, the Romans could have taken it any time. They didn't need to do anything in secret; they ruled most of the known world. In addition, the Roman officials didn't want to do anything that was going to cause more problems with an already unruly and dissatisfied people. The Scriptures point out in Matthew 27:24 that Pilate, as a Roman official, was anxious to resolve the conflict between the Romans and the Jewish leaders over what to do with Jesus Christ.

Needless to say, if the Roman officials had stolen Jesus' body, they would have prolonged, not ended, the political problems with the Jews. Ken Boa and Larry Moody, in their book *I'm Glad You Asked*, show the futility of believing that either the Jews or the Romans stole the body by concluding, "The complete silence on the part of the Jewish and Roman authorities loudly proclaimed their acknowledgment that the body was inexplicably gone."

Day 20

When the chief priests had met with the elders and devised a plan, they gave the soldiers a large sum of money, telling them, "You are to say, 'His disciples came during the night and stole him away while we were asleep.' "

Matthew 28:12–13

According to Matthew 28:12–13, what was the explanation for the empty tomb?

_____

_____

_____

Who bribed the soldiers to lie about how the body had disappeared?

_____

The theory that the disciples may have stolen the body is the oldest attempt to refute the fact of the Resurrection. At first glance, it's also the easiest to believe. What could have been the disciples' motivation for stealing Jesus' body?

_____

_____

_____

Even though the disciples had more reason to steal the body than any other group, they still had to overcome many obstacles to actually accomplish this feat. What were three of the obstacles confronting the disciples? Circle the best answers.

   a. The Roman guard stationed at the tomb.
   b. The fact that they hadn't eaten lunch.
   c. The one-to-two-ton boulder in front of the tomb.
   d. The Roman seal on the tomb.
   e. The desire to attend the Roman circus going on in Jerusalem.

In addition to these obstacles, the disciples had to overcome their own personalities, which were definitely not suited for this dangerous mission. What two characteristics of the disciples were demonstrated in Matthew 8:25–26?

   1. _____

   2. _____

What other characteristics of the disciples do you see in Matthew 14:26?

_____

Write your understanding of Matthew 15:15–16.

_____

_____

_____

What trait of the disciples came to the surface in Matthew 16:22–23?

_____

At other times, the disciples showed themselves to be jealous, cowardly, and self-centered men—men who were hardly capable of devising and implementing a plan that would risk public humiliation as well as certain death.

The disciples' personalities and backgrounds indicate clearly they would not have conceived or desired to preach and die for a lie even for Jesus whom they loved. Therefore, we can safely conclude that "this risen Jesus of Nazareth" who claimed to be the Son of God did indeed rise from the dead, as He said He would.

Day 21

She went and told those who had been with him and who were mourning and weeping. When they heard that Jesus was alive and that she had seen him, they did not believe it.

Mark 16:10–11

How did the disciples feel after they heard that Jesus was alive again?

_____

_____

_____

With the disciples' previously mentioned characteristics and their response to the news of the Resurrection, they seemed to lack the necessary courage and imagination to take Jesus' body.

However, had the disciples decided to steal the body,

there were still several problems. First of all, the Roman guard stationed in front of the tomb was prepared to die to prevent any tampering with the tomb. Read John 19:23–24. These verses demonstrate how vicious the Romans were. In addition, the Roman soldiers guarding the tomb were well acquainted with the harsh discipline of the army. If they failed in their assignment, they would receive the death penalty. The disciples were no match for these efficient, well-motivated guards.

A second obstacle for the disciples was the stone itself. Although there were enough disciples to move the stone, they couldn't have shoved it away without alerting the guards.

Finally, before Pentecost the disciples are described in the Gospels as fearful. Therefore, the Roman seal would have provided the greatest deterrent to the disciples. The breaking of a Roman seal meant certain death. And the disciples were willing to go to any length to stay alive.

Write your understanding of John 20:6–7.

If the disciples had actually overcome all the other obstacles, then they surely would have been in a hurry to remove the body. However, the body wrappings were left in the tomb—some of them neatly folded. No one who would have attempted to steal the body would have taken the time to unwrap it and then fold some of the wrappings neatly before leaving.

Chrysostom, an early church bishop at Antioch, summed up the problem by saying, "For neither, if any persons had removed the body, would they before doing so have stripped it; nor if any had stolen it, would they have taken the trouble to remove the napkin, and roll it up, and lay it in a place by itself; but how? They would have taken the body as it was. On this account John tells us by anticipation that it was buried with much myrrh, which glues linen to the body not less firmly than lead . . ."

Day 22

I tell you the truth, when you were younger you dressed yourself and went out where you wanted; but when you are old you will stretch out your hands, and someone else will dress you and lead you where you do not want to go.

John 21:18

Write your understanding of the significance of John 21:18.

_____

_____

_____

If you had problems understanding this verse, read John 21:19.

This was a prophecy foretelling Peter's death by crucifixion. It is significant because eleven out of twelve disciples were killed for preaching that Jesus Christ was resurrected from the dead. (See Appendix B for more details on how each of the disciples died.) Why would these men willingly die for their beliefs? Circle the most correct answer.

   a. They couldn't outrun the authorities.
   b. Their heating bill was overdue.
   c. They believed that Jesus was the Son of God and that He rose from the dead.
   d. All of the above.
   e. None of the above.
   f. Both a & b.

In what do you believe most strongly? _____

Would you die for this belief? _____

Why do you feel this way?

_____

_____

_____

_____

All over the world people have been put to death for their beliefs. Some beliefs were valid; some were lies. However, everyone who died for a belief sincerely thought he or she was dying for the truth. No one dies for something he or she *knows* to be a lie. Why is this significant?

_____

_____

_____

Day 23

While they were still talking about this, Jesus himself stood among them and said to them, "Peace be with you." They were startled and frightened, thinking they saw a ghost. He said to them, "Why are you troubled, and why do doubts rise in your minds? Look at my hands and my feet. It is I myself! Touch me and see; a ghost does not have flesh and bones, as you see I have."

Luke 24:36–39

In a court trial, who has the greatest influence on the jury? (Circle the best answer.)

a. A scary prosecuting attorney
b. An eloquent defense lawyer
c. Reliable eyewitnesses
d. The court secretary

In the preceding chapters, you have examined the logic of the arguments for and against the Resurrection as the reason that the tomb was empty. However, a truly empty tomb is not the only argument for the literal resurrection of Jesus Christ. The second proof includes Christ's recorded appearances after His crucifixion, death, and burial. Obviously, reliable eyewitnesses are important in deciding what the truth is. With this in mind, match the following with the letter in front of the verse.

Who saw Him	**Where found**
_____ Paul	a. Matthew 28:1–10
_____ Two Women	b. Acts 1:2–3
_____ Five Hundred Witnesses	c. Mark 16:14
_____ Many Women	d. John 20:19–25
_____ One Woman	e. 1 Corinthians 15:8
_____ Eleven Disciples	f. Matthew 28:16–17
_____ Two Men	g. John 21:2
_____ Eleven Disciples	h. Mark 16:9
_____ Seven Disciples	i. 1 Corinthians 15:6
_____ Apostles	j. Mark 16:12
_____ Ten Disciples	k. Luke 24:10
_____ James	l. 1 Corinthians 15:7

From this list it is easy to see that there were many people who claimed to have seen the resurrected Christ. Even the noted Jewish historian Josephus, who is believed to have lived during the last years of Christ's life, mentioned the Resurrection and that Christ had appeared alive on the third day after the Crucifixion. In your own words, what is the importance of so many people claiming to have seen Christ alive after He had died?

_____

_____

_____

What are three possible explanations of why all these people claimed to have seen Jesus?

1. _____

2. _____

3. _____

As you read tomorrow's Bible study you will learn the explanations.

Day 24

We did not follow cleverly invented stories when we told you about the power and coming of our Lord Jesus Christ, but we were eyewitnesses of his majesty. For he received honor and glory from God the Father when the voice came to him from the Majestic Glory, saying, "This is my Son, whom I love; with him I am well pleased." We ourselves heard this voice that came from heaven when we were with him on the sacred mountain.

2 Peter 1:16–18

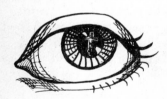

It's clearly understood from the above Scripture that Peter claimed to be an _____ of Jesus Christ's life. The keyword "eyewitness," is used because Peter ate, slept, worked, and lived with Jesus for approximately three years. Therefore, Peter's letters shared a firsthand knowledge about Christ's life. His writings were not based on what was told to a friend of a friend or what was handed down from one generation to another.

However, some critics charge that the Bible is wrong. They state that it doesn't accurately reflect what the eyewitnesses saw. To refute this argument, Nelson Gluek, a renowned

Jewish archaeologist, said, "It may be stated categorically that no archaeological discovery has ever controverted a biblical reference." (*Rivers in the Desert: History of Negev*). All the evidence that has been discovered from historical relics supports the accuracy of the Bible.

Henry Morris, in his book *Many Infallible Proofs*, states, "In view of the unique character of the Bible as well as its incomparable influence for 3,500 years, the testimony of its own writers is of paramount significance. They claimed, of course, that they were writing the words of God. If they really were divinely inspired, then the unique nature and power of the Bible is easily understood. If not, however—if they were either lying or deluded—then we are confronted with the greatest mystery and paradox in all history. One way or the other, the Bible is utterly inexplicable in terms of criteria applicable to other writings."

A second charge concerning the eyewitness accounts is that the witnesses lied about what occurred during Christ's life. However, this wouldn't be logical since eleven of the twelve disciples died for what they claimed to have seen as eyewitnesses. As stated in the study from Day 22, people don't die for what they know to be a lie. Many people die for lies, but they believe them to be truth. If the disciples had lied, they wouldn't have been willing to die for their lie.

A third charge claims that the eyewitnesses were hallucinating. In your opinion, what causes hallucinations?

_____

_____

_____

According to Ken Boa and Larry Moody, in their book *I'm Glad You Asked,* there are some characteristics common to hallucinations:

1. They tend to happen to individuals—not to groups. How does the biblical account differ? (See Matthew 28:16–17; Mark 16:14; John 20:19–25; 1 Corinthians 15:6–7.) _____

_____

2. They tend to reoccur over long periods of time. How does the biblical account differ? (See Acts 1:3; Acts 1:9–11.) _____

_____

3. They occur in people expecting a particular event or person. How does the biblical account differ? (See Luke 24:37; Mark 16:8; Luke 24:11; John 20:25.) _____

_____

4. There tends to be little variety in occurrence. In other words, the same hallucination tends to happen over and over again. How does the biblical account differ? (See John 20:19; John 20:27, John 21:1–4; Luke 24:13–32.) _____

_____

Day 25

Many have undertaken to draw up an account of the things that have been fulfilled among us, just as they were handed down to us by those who from the first were eyewitnesses and servants of the word. Therefore, since I myself have carefully investigated everything from the beginning, it seemed good also to me to write an orderly account for you, most excellent Theophilus, so that you may know the certainty of the things you have been taught.

Luke 1:1—4

 In Luke 1:4, Luke gives the purpose for writing his gospel. Write it out in your own words.

_____

_____

_____

Obviously, Luke didn't believe that all he experienced during and after Christ's life was merely a hallucination or a mental miscalculation on his part.

In yesterday's Bible study it was pointed out that some very common characteristics surround hallucinations. As you discovered from Scripture, these characteristics were not present in the accounts of the sighting of Jesus Christ after His death.

In review, remember that while hallucinations generally occur to individuals, Jesus appeared at least seven times to groups of people. Visions tend to recur over periods of time, but Jesus appeared for forty days and then was gone. A fantasized appearance usually comes to people who are fervently desiring and expecting an appearance. But no one was more surprised by Christ's appearances than His disciples.

Describe the reactions of Christ's friends and disciples on seeing Him:

Luke 24:37 _____

_____

Mark 16:8 _____

_____

Luke 24:11 _____

_____

John 20:25 _____

_____

Luke 24:13–31 _____

_____

John 20:15–16 _____

_____

John 21:4 _____

_____

Finally, while there is little variety in the occurrence of hallucinations, there was great variety in the recorded appearances of Christ. These include Christ talking with people, walking with them, eating, fishing, helping others, and even teaching. In addition, after the forty days, Christ ascended into heaven after appearing to a crowd of almost five hundred (1 Corinthians 15:6—8).

Day 26

But he denied it. "Woman, I don't know him," he said. A little later someone else saw him and said, "You also are one of them." "Man, I am not!" Peter replied. About an hour later another asserted, "Certainly this fellow was with him, for he is a Galilean." Peter replied, "Man, I don't know what you're talking about!" Just as he was speaking, the rooster crowed. The Lord turned and looked straight at Peter. Then Peter remembered the word the Lord had spoken to him: "Before the rooster crows today, you will disown me three times." And he went outside and wept bitterly.

Luke 22:57–60

Another obstacle for doubters of the literal bodily resurrection of Jesus Christ is the drastically changed lives of the disciples once they became convinced that He had actually risen from the dead. Someone or something must be responsible for the remarkable change that occurred in the lives of these ordinary men. (See Appendix B for more details on how each of the disciples died for preaching Jesus' resurrection.)

On the next page, circle the verse you're reading and then draw a line to the pre-resurrection characteristic of the disciples that is best demonstrated by the verse.

81

Luke 24:38	Lacking understanding
Mark 10:35–37	Stumbling block
Matthew 16:22–23	Doubting
Matthew 26:73–74	Ambitious
Luke 8:25	Cowardly
Mark 9:32	Fearful
Matthew 20:22–24	Jealous
Mark 4:40	Little faith
Matthew 16:8	Timid
Mark 6:52	Hardened heart

You can see from these characteristics and what you learned in Day 20 that no one would have picked these men to lead a revolution. But Jesus Christ saw their inner qualities and was convinced that once He had risen from the dead, these disciples would go to any lengths to share His gospel with others, even to the point of laying down their lives. This is the only explanation that is logical enough to explain how these timid men went out and changed the world.

Day 27

Many have undertaken to draw up an account of the things that have been fulfilled among us, just as they were handed down to us by those who from the first were eyewitnesses and servants of the word. Therefore, since I myself have carefully investigated everything from the beginning, it seemed good also to me to write an orderly account for you, most excellent Theophilus, so that you may know the certainty of the things you have been taught.

Luke 1:1–4

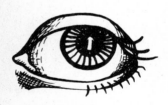

Put yourself in the disciples' place. If you had seen Jesus beaten, whipped, crucified, and buried, what would have convinced you to be willing to die for preaching Jesus' resurrection?

_____

_____

_____

_____

Reread the Scripture for today. Again, the key word used by Luke is _____ . Something happened to drastically change the disciples forever. According to Luke 1:1–4, they were eyewitnesses from the beginning of Christ's ministry. This ministry included His rising from the dead. Christ knew that it was very important that His disciples actually see Him alive after His death. Write your understanding of Luke 24:45–48.

_____

_____

_____

Christ stated that because the disciples were witnesses to all that had happened, they should go out and tell the world so that everyone might believe in Christ as the Living Redeemer of all mankind.

Would it be easier for you to believe if you had been one of the disciples? Why?

_____

_____

_____

_____

What was the name of the disciple who was nicknamed "the doubter" (John 20:24)?

_____

In John 20:25, this disciple said, "Unless I see the nail marks in his hands and put my finger where the nails were, and put my hand into his side, I will not believe it." What happened in John 20:26-28?

_____

_____

_____

Although Christ recognized the importance of the disciples' faith after they had seen Him alive, He stated that those who found Him another way would receive a special blessing. Write what you think John 20:29 means.

_____

_____

_____

Day 28

Jesus asked the boy's father, "How long has he been like this?" "From childhood," he answered. "It has often thrown him into fire or water to kill him. But if you can do anything, take pity on us and help us." " 'If you can'?" said Jesus. "Everything is possible for him who believes." Immediately the boy's father exclaimed, "I do believe; help me overcome my unbelief!"

Mark 9:21—24

What is the meaning of the above Scripture?

_____

_____

_____

Although the father was struggling with whether he believed that Jesus could help his son, he mustered enough faith and courage to tell Jesus that he wanted to believe. But he needed Christ's help. Your faith is much the same. Christ is looking for that desire in you that wants to believe.

Some of you might have stated in yesterday's study that it would have been easier for you to believe in Jesus Christ if you had actually seen Him performing His miracles. Rethink this question as you read John 11:11–44 and summarize what happened.

_____

_____

_____

_____

There doesn't appear to be much discussion over what took place here. With many witnesses present, both believers and nonbelievers, Christ raised a man from the dead who had been buried for _____ days (John 11:17).

Many people stop here in this magnificent and miraculous account of Jesus' compassion for people and His power over death. However, the story continues in the next chapter of John where the nonbelievers' reactions to Lazarus are evident. Read John 12:9–11, and write down their reactions.

_____

_____

_____

As you can see, the problem with the chief priests' disbelief was not lack of evidence. The greatest miracle that they would ever see was living in Bethany. The chief priests' unbelief was caused by their stubbornness and pride. What was the chief priests' reason for wanting to kill Lazarus (John 12:11)?

_____

_____

_____

   Much like the chief priests, some of you may be struggling
with your stubbornness and pride in relationship to Jesus
Christ's claims. Don't allow these characteristics to cloud the
facts. Reread Mark 9:24 and write out the father's request.
This should be your request as well.

_____

_____

_____

   If there are excuses or reasons keeping you from believing in Jesus, list them here:

   1. _____

   2. _____

   3. _____

Day 29

Now fear the LORD and serve him with all faithfulness. Throw away the gods your forefathers worshiped beyond the River and in Egypt, and serve the LORD. But if serving the LORD seems undesirable to you, then choose for yourselves this day whom you will serve, whether the gods your forefathers served beyond the River, or the gods of the Amorites, in whose land you are living. But as for me and my household, we will serve the LORD.

Joshua 24:14–15

God has been giving mankind the same choice throughout history. According to Joshua 24:15, what is the choice?

_____

_____

God didn't want you to be a simple robot—He gave you the option of choosing to serve Him or choosing not to. However, as experience has shown, every option has consequences. Some of the consequences are good; others are terrible. It depends on the choice that's made. The Bible declares that you must, "Choose this day whom you will serve."

When God was dealing with Israel, He clearly laid out the choices and the consequences. In Deuteronomy 28:1-2, God said if you will _____ _____ then He will set you _____ _____ all the nations of the earth. What does verse 2 say will come upon the Israelites if they obey the Lord?

_____

That was the "good news." The "bad news" shows up in Deuteronomy 28:15-19. If the people chose not to _____ the Lord, then what would overtake them?

_____

To make a wise choice in your relationship to Jesus Christ, read and apply Proverbs 9:10: "The fear of the LORD is the beginning of wisdom, and knowledge of the Holy One is understanding." God has pointed out that the choice of following Him is one that is filled with wisdom and knowledge.

It's not a decision that's made after you know everything there is to know about God, because you never reach that position. It's a decision that's made based on the evidence at hand. This is not just a decision that was given to the Israelites during Joshua's time. It's a decision that has been given to you today. God is waiting for your answer.

C.S. Lewis, in his book *Mere Christianity*, clearly explains the decision: "A man who was merely a man and said the sort of things Jesus said would not be a great moral teacher. He would either be a lunatic—on a level with the man who says he is a poached egg—or else he would be the Devil of Hell. You must make your choice. Either this man was, and is, the Son of God: or else a madman or something worse. You can shut Him up for a fool; you can spit at Him and kill Him as a demon; or you can fall at His feet and call Him Lord and God. But let us not come with any patronizing nonsense about His being a great human teacher. He has not left that open to us."

Today I choose (a) to be a follower of Christ (b) not to be a follower of Christ (circle one) because

_____

_____

_____

_____

Day 30

If I fought wild beasts in Ephesus for merely human reasons, what have I gained? If the dead are not raised, "Let us eat and drink, for tomorrow we die."

1 Corinthians 15:32

 Through your reading of the past few Bible studies, you have learned from Scripture that Jesus' tomb was empty and that Jesus predicted before His death that He would rise from the dead.

In the above Scripture, Paul states that if Jesus didn't conquer death, then Christians have no hope. They might as well get whatever they can out of life because there is nothing good after death.

Certainly many people have chosen the philosophy of life mentioned in verse 32. "Eat, drink, and be merry for tomorrow we die." This characterizes the philosophy known as *hedonism.* Another way of explaining this philosophy is, "If it feels good, do it!"

On the other hand, Paul teaches in 1 Corinthians 15 that because Christ rose from the dead, all who are in Christ (Christians) will likewise conquer death and be raised from the grave. (For what it means to be a Christian, please see Appendix A.)

Your eternal destination (as well as that of everyone else) is based on how you respond to the risen Christ. In Romans 4:22–25, Paul states that Christ's resurrection is _____ proof:

    a. fairly good
    b. positive
    c. bad

of God's acceptance of the sacrifice made by Jesus Christ for the sins of _____ of mankind.

    a. most
    b. some
    c. none
    d. all

Furthermore, Jesus' resurrection demonstrates that He is powerful enough to do the same for everyone who will believe and follow Him. How has the resurrection of Jesus Christ affected your life:

at home? _____

at school? _____

at work? _____

at church? _____

with Christian friends? _____

_____

with non-Christian friends? _____

_____

in dating/marriage? _____

_____

in your attitudes toward yourself? _____

_____

If you have not yet become a Christian, how would the resurrection of Jesus Christ affect your life after you made that commitment?

_____

_____

_____

Day 31

"But what about you?" he asked. "Who do you say I am?" Simon Peter answered, "You are the Christ, the Son of the living God." Jesus replied, "Blessed are you, Simon son of Jonah, for this was not revealed to you by man, but by my Father in heaven."

Matthew 16:15—17

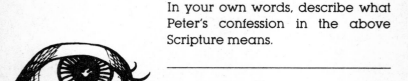

In your own words, describe what Peter's confession in the above Scripture means.

_____

_____

_____

Through much of this Bible study, you have examined the evidence surrounding the Crucifixion and the Resurrection as if you were looking through Peter's eyes. However, now you must arrive at your own conclusions from the available evidence.

In summary:

1. Legal-historical proof and scientific proof are equally valid.
2. Experience dictates that you ask for an amount of proof that is beyond a reasonable doubt (not beyond the shadow of doubt).
3. Historians agree that Jesus hung on a cross and was buried in a tomb.
4. Historians also agree that the tomb was empty three days after the crucifixion.
5. There are basically four arguments as to why the tomb was empty:
   a. *Swoon Theory* (see Days 13–17).
   b. *Wrong Tomb Theory* (see Day 18).
   c. *Stolen Body Theory* (see Days 19–22).
   d. *Resurrection Theory* (Jesus actually rose from the dead).
6. In addition to the empty tomb, there are many recorded appearances of Jesus after His resurrection (see Days 23–25).
7. The lives of the disciples were changed radically (see Days 26–27).

With the above summary and the conscientious study of this book in mind, circle the number that best describes your convictions of how *YOU* view the literal bodily resurrection of Jesus Christ:

I strongly disagree	I disagree	I'm not sure	I agree	I strongly agree
1 2	3 4	5 6 7	8 9	10

Now write a short note to a friend defending or explaining the response you circled. Be specific.

Dear _____,
   I believe / don't believe (circle the correct one for you) in the resurrection of Jesus Christ from the dead because _____

_____

_____

_____

_____

_____

_____

_____

_____

_____

Sincerely,

_____
(your name)

___, ___, ___
(date)

Appendix A

God loves you and desires to give you peace, joy, and eternity in heaven.

What You Need to Know:

1. God loves you and has a wonderful gift for you.

   "For God so loved the world that he gave his one and only Son, that whoever believes in him shall not perish but have eternal life" (John 3:16).

   "For the wages of sin is death, but the gift of God is eternal life in Christ Jesus our Lord" (Romans 6:23).

2. You cannot obtain this gift of eternal life on your own.

   "He saved us, not because of righteous things we had done, but because of his mercy" (Titus 3:5).

   "For it is by grace you have been saved, through faith—and this not from yourselves, it is the gift of God—not by works, so that no one can boast" (Ephesians 2:8–9).

3. You need to come into a right relationship with God to receive this gift of eternal life.

   "I tell you the truth, no one can see the kingdom of God unless he is born again" (John 3:3).

"I tell you the truth, whoever hears my word and believes him who sent me has eternal life and will not be condemned" (John 5:24).

4. God sent Jesus Christ to be your way to experience forgiveness of sins and eternal life.

"God made him who had no sin to be sin for us, so that in him we might become the righteousness of God" (2 Corinthians 5:21).

"For there is one God and one mediator between God and men, the man Christ Jesus, who gave himself as a ransom for all men" (1 Timothy 2:5–6).

"For Christ died for sins once for all, the righteous for the unrighteous, to bring you to God" (1 Peter 3:18).

5. God's time for you to receive this gift is *now*.

"I tell you, now is the time of God's favor, now is the day of salvation" (2 Corinthians 6:2).

"Do not boast about tomorrow, for you do not know what a day may bring forth" (Proverbs 27:1).

What You Need to Do:

1. Admit you have a need. ("I am a sinner.")

"There is no one who does good, not even one" (Romans 3:12).

"All have sinned and fall short of the glory of God" (Romans 3:23).

"For whoever keeps the whole law and yet stumbles at just one point is guilty of breaking all of it" (James 2:10).

2. Acknowledge that Jesus Christ died for you on the cross, rose from the dead, and is today with God the Father in Heaven. ("I believe Jesus Christ is the Son of God, and He alone can provide salvation for me.")

   "Salvation is found in no one else, for there is no other name under heaven given to men by which we must be saved" (Acts 4:12).

   "That if you confess with your mouth, 'Jesus is Lord,' and believe in your heart that God raised him from the dead, you will be saved. For it is with your heart that you believe and are justified, and it is with your mouth that you confess and are saved" (Romans 10:9–10).

3. Affirm your belief in Jesus by inviting Him to come in and forgive you of your sins and control every area of your life. ("I receive Jesus Christ as my Savior and Lord.")

   "Here I am! I stand at the door and knock. If anyone hears my voice and opens the door, I will come in and eat with him, and he with me" (Revelation 3:20).

   "Yet to all who received him, to those who believed in his name, he gave the right to become children of God" (John 1:12).

What You Need to Pray:

Dear God,

I admit that I am a sinner. Please forgive me of all my sins and help me to be what You want me to be from this moment on.

Jesus, I now invite You to come into my life. Thank You for dying on the cross for me so that I could have eternal life. I put my complete trust in You alone for eternal life.

Thank You for coming into my heart and saving me now. In Jesus' name. Amen.

What You Need to Remember:

If you prayed this prayer, you have just begun a meaningful and new life with Jesus Christ. To experience God's *best* in your Christian life, you need to:

B— Begin reading and applying the Bible each day to help you know Jesus better.

E— Every day talk to God your Father in prayer. Be open and honest.

S— Share your faith in Christ with others. Start right now.

T— Take time to attend a church where you can learn more about how to grow as a Christian and can fellowship with other Christians.

Appendix B

The Disciples as Martyrs

The following list of early Church leaders and disciples was taken from *Fox's Book of Martyrs.*

1. Stephen—stoned to death at Jerusalem.
2. James* the son of Zebedee—beheaded in Judea.
3. Philip–scourged, thrown into prison, and then crucified in Upper Asia.
4. Matthew–killed by a weapon with an axlike cutting blade in Ethiopia.
5. James* the son of Alphaeus—at age ninety-four, beaten and stoned and had his brains dashed out with a fuller's club in Jerusalem.
6. Matthias–stoned and then beheaded at Jerusalem.
7. Andrew–crucified on an especially cruel type of cross (at Edessa), which has been named a St. Andrew cross.
8. Mark—dragged to pieces in Greece.
9. Peter–crucified upside down in Rome.
10. Paul—beheaded in Rome.
11. Thaddaeus* (Jude)—crucified at Edessa.
12. Bartholomew–cruelly beaten and then crucified in India.
13. Thomas–killed by a spear in India.
14. Luke—hung by the neck in Britain.
15. Simon–crucified in Britain.

*Indicates the disciples.

16. John—the only disciple to escape martyrdom; however, after he was thrown into a pot of boiling oil and miraculously escaped, he was banished to the deserted Isle of Patmos.

Appendix C

Suggested Reading

Boa, Kenneth, and Larry Moody. *I'm Glad You Asked.* Wheaton: Victor Books, 1982.

*DeWitt, David. *Answering the Tough Ones.* Chicago: Moody Press, 1982.

*Little, Paul. *Know Why You Believe.* Wheaton: Victor Books, 1978.

*McDowell, Josh. *More than a Carpenter.* Wheaton: Tyndale House, 1977.

Morison, Frank. *Who Moved the Stone?* Grand Rapids: Zondervan, 1977.

*This book is a little easier reading than the others suggested.